Under the Sea

Written by Sarah O'Neil

Contents

Introduction

Water covers more than four-fifths of the earth's surface. Most of this water is found in the seas and oceans. It is salty water.

Some plants and animals are able to live in salty water. The sea is a rich source of food for many things.

Seaweed

Seaweed is a plant that can live in the sea. Seaweed can be red, brown, or green. Some seaweeds can float in the water. Others attach themselves to the ocean floor or other solid objects.

Unlike most land plants, seaweeds do not take up food through their roots. Instead they absorb food from the water.

Californian kelp is a kind of seaweed.

Close-up
of the balls
that help
Californian
kelp to
float

Like most plants, seaweed
can make its own food
from sunlight.

Some seaweeds have small
balls that help them float
up to the surface to reach
the sunlight.

7

Coral

Coral can look like a plant. But it really is made up of millions of tiny animals called coral polyps.

Coral polyps live in coral colonies. They eat tiny animals that they catch and poison.

When the polyps die, their skeletons form the reef on which other polyps live.

Gorgonian coral – each of the "flowers" is a coral polyp.

A coral reef

Fish

Fish are animals that live in the sea.
They are able to breathe under water.
They can be any size, from tiny to huge.

Butterfly fish are small fish. The largest ones are only 8 inches (20 centimeters) long.

Fish with sharp teeth eat animals.
Some fish eat plants. Others filter
small floating plants from the water.

A great white
shark can grow
up to 36 feet
(11 meters)
in length.

11

Mammals

Whales and dolphins are mammals. They spend all of their lives in the water, but swim to the surface to breathe air. If a whale or dolphin is not able to swim to the surface, it will drown.

Some whales feed on schools of fish. Other whales feed on tiny floating sea creatures called krill. Dolphins mostly catch individual fish or squid.

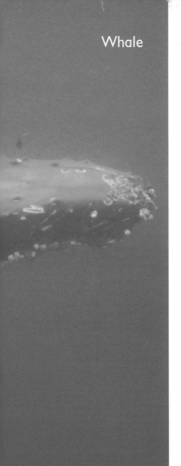

Whale

Sea otter

Sea otters are mammals, too. They spend most of their lives in the sea. They eat fish and other sea animals, such as crabs and clams.

Sea otters sleep, mate, and give birth to their young in the water.

13

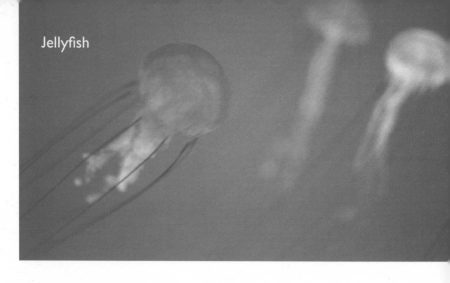

Jellyfish

Jellyfish and Sea Anemones

Jellyfish move through the water with poisonous tentacles floating behind them. If a smaller animal touches a tentacle, it is poisoned, and the jellyfish may eat it.

Some animals, such as sea anemones, look like plants. They hold onto rocks and wait for food to come by. When food touches them, they quickly grab and eat the animal.

14

Sea anemone

15

Sea Crustaceans

Crabs, lobsters, and shrimp are crustaceans. They have an external skeleton and limbs with joints. Crustaceans eat small plants and animals.

Crustaceans have many legs, which help them to move about in the sea. Most crustaceans use their tails for swimming and can move backward to escape danger.

Crab

limbs with joints

external skeleton

Conclusion

Many different plants and animals live in the sea. They depend on its water and other living things to stay alive. They have found different ways to protect themselves and to find food.

Reef fish

Shell-less
mollusk

19

Index